Megan Mccorquodale

What
I
Told
Frank

CLOCHODERICK

What I Told Frank was first published in 2018
by Clochoderick Press.
First Edition.
www.clochoderickpress.co.uk

Clochoderick Press
27 Newton Street
Paisley
Renfrewshire
Scotland
PA1 2RN

A CIP catalogue record for this book is available from the British Library.

ISBN: 978-1-912345-06-9

Typeset by R.K. Wallace in Garamond 12pt

Printed and bound by:
Imprint Academic
Seychelles Farm, Upton Pyne, Exeter, Devon EX5 5HY

Funded by:

Acknowledgements

This book came from a lot of my darkest places, but I needed them as much as I needed this, so I am thankful for this opportunity to push myself to create something I wanted as much as I needed it.

I'd have more acknowledgements than poems if I listed everyone I wanted to thank, so I'd just like to thank everyone who provided me with, and were involved in, all of my experiences (good and bad) that gave me something to write about.

I want to thank R.K. Wallace of Clochoderick Press, who has been reading and editing my work and drinking wine with me for a long time before the opportunity for me to be published came around, so thank you for encouraging me to write this collection and all of the work you have done to make this possible.

Lastly, I'd like to thank Billy Liar for taking time out to read this and write the beautiful words on the back of this book, thank you for making me feel understood.

Contents

AMSTERDAM

the night burnt out
like many of my favourite musicians
while the sky didn't hesitate
to become bubble gum morning blue
there was no evidence of the darkness
as I cradled my aches
along a street I didn't know
in Amsterdam

I let my fingers brush along
rusted paint flaking lamp posts
and I wondered what they had seen
in a city like this
the morning breeze
was the only thing holding down
my stomach acid

I know that existential fear
is inside all of us
waiting to shatter us like
a body compressed in outer space
but this has plagued me
followed me around
until I almost feel like I'm fading
when I'd always wanted to burn out

I sat on the bench with only
two wooden planks
and stared off into the canal covered in ice
ignoring the phone call
to tell me our flight was in a few hours
I didn't think I'd ever be ready to go back

so I made a deal with myself
in a street I didn't know
in a city where I'd abandon my own soul
I promised I wouldn't fade away
if I was going to be around
if this was going to be my comeback story

I would always want to burn out

THIS IS ALL HYPOTHETICAL

I want to tell you
about the night that hasn't happened yet
how we lean out of windows
we aren't supposed to
shoulder to shoulder just for a cigarette

we're fully dressed
because I'm still not comfortable
standing naked by myself
never mind in front of you yet
even though
my words have read to you
all of my vulnerabilities
it felt close enough for me

though I can't deny I love the frost
of your fingers along the back of my neck
and up to my ears
ones that were left to hang out of the window
like a foot between coming and going
I think it's just a metaphor
for both our feet stuck in this door
of us

over a skyline of stone and concrete
we can both admire
I'm not sure what we've been talking about
because honestly when I'm drunk
it's Jekyll and Hyde
you never know what you're going to get
but in a lottery of long nights
I'd hope in this one I was kind

that we would have exhausted the nights hours
ones where you promise me
a walk in the streets
we've both seen so many times
at 2am
but you explain how different they can look
over a dying sunset
a pint and a thunderstorm of rain

that's the difference between us
when we describe our opposite sides of the day
in our bodies Morse code
I'll do it on a worn couch with the way
I kiss in Sunday morning lust
it will paint you the sunrise
where your hands instead
are the violence of colours
colliding together
just to set me on fire
the only comfort I can take from it
is that like our tobacco and rolling papers
we'll burn together
in a sunset bonfire of this

though that is all hypothetical
the two of us
tucked away in a back bar
clinging to drinks
that taste more familiar for now
than your mouth ever will

GLASGOW

the drink in my hand feels the same
the bitter taste of it on my tongue
making my skin goosebumps
feels the same
only it's one pound and forty nine pence
more than I'm used to

feeling this lack of change in my hand
reminds me of the way
my tongue runs over a missing tooth
this occasional algorithm pain of home
echoes now in halls
that no longer bare my portraits

so I can empathise with her body
how she has changed so much
with only brick and stone to remind her
of who she was
of all those who inhabited her
now laid to rest in her concrete rib-cage
and I told us both it was okay to rebuild ourselves
but you can only bleed your lungs and knuckles
into brick and stone for so long
before it destroys one of us
or both of us

I took a train today
wondering what it was like to go missing
how it would feel
to wake up in the middle of the night
kiss her from the other side of the door
and just go

out into the darkness
of her streets that made me forget
just how big the world is

and maybe I only reached Edinburgh
a pub on the Cowgate
but maybe going missing
isn't just about leaving
maybe going missing
is about being made of
bones neurons struggling breaths
and nothing else

so I'm not finished here yet
admitting the problem is only the first step
and there is something to be said
about being a stow away in a city that relies on its history
but doesn't know a page of mine

somewhere I can let myself laugh and breathe
admist blue smoke for the first time in weeks
outside where a yellow box of matches
passes between our strange rough hands
somewhere I can finally admit
I can no longer be monogamist for the sake of my home city

I'm tired
and I wish there was more I could say before I go
I wish it didn't have to be this way
I'm sorry
Glasgow

MUSICIAN'S FINGERTIPS

I cant seem to shake this
maudlin state of mind
when I'm seeking inspiration
from the dark
of musicians beds

seeking out the callous'
of their fingertips
along the hip bones
of a cathedral body
empty of prayers
laying mesmerised
by the way they smoke their cigarettes
watching as they draw
their life source from fire
and unresolved angst
just so that I can know
in the middle of the night
my hauntings
wouldn't frighten you too
because god knows
there have been so many before you

who don't know how I worry for myself in peace time
because I have never had the choice
to be a pacifist
I'm not sure how to unbind my fists
how to not be ready to throw the first punch
when I'm as fragile as stained glass windows
that are already missing pieces
but books in between bottles in the kitchen
gave me the sermon of Little Annie

which resonated in my restless disposition
to the punk philosophy
that it might not just be me
who hates myself
exhume somewhere
where we can create a hunt for any other
definition for what they taught us
when I know that my soul
will only speak with the others who are lost

that philosophy
and those words you bleed from
a stained chest of
cynicism and regret
you'll hear me
sing them back to you
just so that you know
what's inside of you
wouldn't frighten me
or make me leave
because god knows
there have already been so many before me

FRANK CALLS WHEN IT RAINS

Frank calls when it rains
I mean really raining
when you can watch it
bounce on pot-holed ground
water trodden into the road
through thick winter soles

Frank tells me I have a winter soul
I say it's an act of rebellion
to my summer birth right
but that it rains every year
on my birthday anyway
so what does it matter

I wonder about that often
about the dates I have subconsciously
ingrained into the grounds
of my traumatised unconscious
so that on some of them I cant leave the house

Frank tells me I have every reason
to be warmer now
that ice doesn't have to trap
me
the way it did in that flat
we lived in
where I finally gave in

I say I'd rather trap myself
behind a bar
or in dragging my nails
down someone else's chest
scalding myself through words
that if I said them out loud
would betray their own body
I say I'm not sure
I want to feel anything yet

though I wonder
in the silent breathless moments
of a radio silence
between telephone lines
just how I would go about
feeling again
especially on days like today
when I hold myself hostage
to clockwork
something entirely man made
yet she is the reason it is frozen
for twenty four hours every year
because its the eleventh of March
again

Frank calls when it rains
I say its not raining outside today
but Frank calls anyway

FORTY TWO MILES

my friends laugh when they see
the array of wine bottles next to my sofa
but they don't know why I keep them around
that they are there completely on purpose
not because Merlot was how we
chanced a nervous first kiss
but because they remind me of you
of us
better than any photograph could

maybe because they form a trail
like the warpath of our clothes
from the front door
to the bedroom floor
but this time
when we are finished looking for each others borders
any foreign skin is now familiar
the taste of your mouth is as craved
as a morning cigarette

yet you are forty two miles away
in a city that breathes through stone
who's spires have watched hundreds
of Hogmanay fireworks
who's streets are trampled every day
by tourists
I'd hope by now I no longer am one
when we trace your paths
of the past years of a life
making my own place here
where we can just worry about the weather together

though it's more about what they cant see
the feeling ruins me like a fever
like a fire hazard for lit match hands
it's engulfing it's desperate
when we find a quiet moment
a quiet street
any second that having you close to me
means the world isn't falling down on top of us
or when time isn't pushing us to either side of the country
I would take this coast and pull it towards me as easily as
the bed sheets
that cloak our skin in bed's with high or low ceilings
where our mouths have met more often than we have

because of those forty two miles
the hour and fifteen minutes on a bus
or forty five minutes if we can afford a train
but the weight of you in bed next to me
makes me wish that you'll never be that far again
that maybe one day
you'll only be as far as the line
of wine bottles
at the side of my sofa

4:20AM

cold stiff sheets
meets hands blue
that slide across star years
till cold stiff hands
meets warm flesh
that moulds like clay
into the shape that cradles our delicate frames

though there are few mornings
where skin is touched carelessly
and burned like hot radiators
or candles
that if forgotten in sleep
will burn down the house
overnight

but it is the heat of nightmares
that fresh sting
that steals us from the tight hold of sleep
to an empty bed instead
as barren as an apocalyptic wasteland
no fingertips stained skin from ink
to share with notebooks nearby

last nights vices
leave the rotten taste in our mouths
though the morning no longer sighs
like the night under the weight
of raised voices

then morning breaks
the sun rises
and any recollection
of the friction between sheets
the hot coals of bodies
on a pyre
is just two pale cages of brittle bones
in a cold iron bed at 4:20am

EMPTY SPACES

they called it ablution
washing all the glass out of the cuts in the sink
I wish we could wash away our sins
from the outside
like they reside merely on the surface of our skin

while I hang in the empty space
· behind the bar
singing with the clinking and smashes of
bottles at my back
my body aches
if not from being on my feet all night
then from the alcohol abuse
that has turned my skin grey
my bones too weak to hold myself up
but this is deep rooted
I am now a catacomb
for only blood and alcohol

numbness and stupidity
when I'm at my weakest
are the reasons I punch walls
only for it to prove
to my bloodied knuckles
just how weak I am against it

weaker than the days
I'm haunting the only good soul
I have seen not stained yet with my sins
as he has to drag me out of bed
and hold me up to the sunlight

to remind me that I'm not translucent
that I exist in this world
and tomorrow is going to happen
whether I want to fight or not

but in these empty spaces
with pint glasses cradled in old hands
and old mouths silenced by the same exhaustion
I think too much
about how you are in every mistake I make
you are every man I let touch me
not because I wanted it
but because sometimes everything just hurts
you are the deep rooted aching
for the alcohol in my bloodstream

You are every pain as
I'm burying the sharp part of my key
into the palm of my fist
while I bury the thought of you in the pit of my stomach
far down from the heart that's in my throat
You were every bruise I wanted to feel
because somewhere along the line
its had it's use
The feeling of my pulse aching
behind the black and blue

because then I can at least feel something

NAUSEA

have you ever seen cracks in the pavement
as if the flowers are strong enough to push through con-
crete
that it is nature who made those cracks
but its cynical ideas that bring us back
to realising that nature
is only as permanent as we allow it to be
and all of those cracks
that exist on our own skin
in our skulls
are just as man made
as the ones on the pavement

we are just as permanent as nature
but less useful
if you want to be nihilistic about it
our flowers
aren't enough to break through skin
the way another person can fracture bones
and ideas
without leaving a mark of their own
those kind of insights
someone told me
is what nausea feels like

so I'm drinking hard tonight
hard from the beers
you left in the barren fridges bottom drawer
because I'm feeling sore

talking of sore
I wonder if you are ready for the way my heart aches
how I will break it for you
but how I promise that this pain will cease to manifest
in bars sex or something else
other than these words that will leak out of my mouth
because at this stage in your long lived history
you're probably sick of our poetry

though sometimes
I will be the time you jumped a fence
catching on its sharpened edge
what you thought was your jeans
instead it was tearing at your skin
blood pouring out of you
the way my words do when I'm a little less than sober
too many words that now cannot be unsaid
and spoken so quickly
like the way the sky turned red that night
I think they said this is what nausea feels like

but I'm yet to pin that feeling down
when during a seance of a night we lost hours ago
lying with our hands tangled in the twists of
my metal bed frame
we asked one another if we'd ever seen a ghost before
and I think yours still haunt your hearts chambers
but I wasn't ready to tell you
that most days it's all I see
when I hide in bathrooms
with white walls
and no mirrors

just pale legs balancing on a porcelain sink
when I've had too much to drink
or because sometimes I just cant breathe

despite it all
despite my body brutalised by panic attacks
and intrusive thoughts
that ransack anything close to rationality
I'll never stop apologising for my self
destructive self medication
but I want you to know
I wrote this last stanza happy
because though I struggle
not to hate some of these man made things
I could never hate you

FLESH CAN FILL A ROOM

I've seen the inside of hospital rooms
far too often in my life
than I should have
I can still smell the bleach
that tries to cover the stench
of just that
ghosts and triers
and I'm not sure when I stopped being a ghost
or if I ever have

maybe that's why now
instead of going
to a hospital on top of the hill
I'll clean my wounds
with vodka
and call it salt water
because how can a doctor
repair me from the inside
without my identity
becoming a hospital gown

that's why I've tried
not to carve your name into
my graveyard chest
because
I'm trying to stop myself
begging for someone to make me better
I've done it alone
long enough now to know
that anyone who will lick my wounds
will be poisoned by
the blood in their mouths

so I'm not asking you for that
Frank
I haven't used my words
to tell anyone enough of the truth
they are just scarred
with the scraping of the surface

so I cut my nails more often now
while I sit on the kitchen floor
and I'll hold my knees to my chest
making sure I cant tear away at my skin
to ensure I leave something
of my flesh left for you
whenever you decide
to share your secrets
with my skin
and bone
already rattled by my own

I will wait
because flesh can fill a room
when ghosts can't

IT'S NOT THAT I DON'T LOVE YOU

"it's not that I don't love you"
was that an excuse
some broken excuse
like squeezing glass
into the palm of my fist

fuck you
not for not loving me
but because it's Thursday night
so I can count back those days
from Monday
three days
of the however many hours
where you still pretended to love me
before any courage
could push out a truth
I should have already
known

on Monday
when you kissed my nose
smiled at me
and stroked my neck
as if it were muscle memory
tell me if it feels like hers

on Tuesday
when you took the pan handle
in frustration
as water boiled over
hissing at me
she stood in the corner

on Wednesday
you went out into the street
below our window
like any other day
in the past lifetime
that we have lived together
but you were holding her hand
inside yours
as if to hide her
as poorly as you had been

on Thursday
I'd rather shove the bloody broken glass
into my mouth than hear
anything that will come out of yours

WARNING SIGNS

I rub the cold steel
of the bird pin badge
between my finger and thumb
I keep things
people I no longer know
once gave me
to remind myself that
no part of my life
is victim-less

so I want you to know
that I carry those shattered pieces
of a life we could have had
like thorns in my crown
but I'm no messiah
even though everyday
I rise from the dead
out of the mattress
keeping cold sweat records
of my night terrors

and I suppose
I just don't want that to happen to you
while I'm trying to find new ways
to block out the sun
you remind me of every step I take forward
that I know is unstable
on the six drinks I've just thrown back
I can't turn water into wine
but I can sure as hell
alter my blood levels

so I'm sorry that even a pint
can't make it easy
for me to crawl out of the old skin
I should have shed long ago
isn't the sun just too bright?

sometimes I talk in my sleep
funny how unconscious
I'm at my most awake
telling stories that should have left
my throat long before my stomach acid did
so I keep my fingers on cold steel
while my feet move blindly in the familiar pattern
because disassociating in front of bright lights
is far too easy
even if they are artificial

the same way my feelings are glass cabinets
in a museum of trauma
you have yet to explore
so have you ever wondered
if maybe every piece of me
you've seen so far
is just a trick of the light?
I'm sorry sometimes
I'm like this
always setting myself up for an apology
for all of those 3 am words I should never have said
or that these cigarette burns
weren't enough of a warning sign

well at least mine weren't

FIVE PAGE PAMPHLET

have you ever felt yourself just breathing
like your whole body
is incapable of absolutely
anything else
but breathing
every rise and fall of your chest
is an earthquake in your bones
rippling under your skin
you are just numb

and begging to be hit
with something
wishing for the feeling
of at least your heart beating
against your chest
like a fist
because now the fever
has stopped ripping through you
like a wild fire
that has been put out
leaving only smoke bereaving your lungs
with your fifth cigarette
that still hasn't taken away the smell
of wet graveyard grass yet

its just past four
the same way you were late to our first date
it wouldn't be you
if you weren't late to your own funeral
but there is no apology this time
no bad aftershave staining
scarred skin those viking parts of you
that I cant imagine
fit into that wooden box

though this time I'm still looking at my feet
I cant look at it until you are almost gone
I hope they spread you
in the ocean or the mountains
where you belong
I can still feel my knees quake
and I know you would appreciate
the metaphor
of this grief
being the alien waiting to rip its way
out of my chest
or the way the guilt of losing touch this past year
makes my eyes burn
my tired brain begging for you to walk
up behind me

but this rain shattered day of black suits and grey faces
isn't how I want to remember you
In fact the best sex we ever had
was after we argued about the existence of a god
and for a long time I felt like we
weren't kneeling at the same alter
but in the end you told me no matter what
you had met your match with me
so sit back down beside me
pull the curtains closed
on both of us
pass me another glass of rum
and tell me every detail
of how you saw the world
through a view
as poisoned with cynicism as my own
that's how I want to remember you

but staring down the barrel
of a crematorium aisle
I have no choice but to tell you
that these days
I cannot even look at Byres Road
without shaking
the way my hands are now
in this empty space
that you took up
spread out into
a five page pamphlet
that would never do your life justice

so for now you win
I mumble into a blue smoke cloud tonight
when there are no dark teary shadows around
to hear this
I make peace with the sky
because I couldn't make it with you
and before my voice cracks
I ask a god I don't believe in
for a world after this one
so you can tell me
if it's all true

SWEAT RED STRIPE AND CIGARETTES

I found my will to live
at the same punk gig
where I almost broke my ribs
but this tight vacuum
of sweat red-stripe and cigarettes
broke down our fourth wall of lost hours
until you could tell me
how your bones shook
the way mines did
not with the wind
but with what was inside of us

I lost you then
in the heat that was making it's way up
or down
somewhere I lost my hand in your hair
the sweat thick on your forehead
breaking a fever
until we only saw red
red stripe cans the only thing keeping our hands busy
maybe that was a dream
or I was overcome with
the thing that shook us from the inside
until blurry eyes
met something like MDMA sleep

so back into this dream next week
I realise that it was true
meeting you
it was easy to keep it on a pedestal

where you cant see those cracks face to face
while mine are filled with gold
yours are the footsteps I take in a smoky room
yet to be met with anyone else's eyes
but my own

that's why there is too much risk in finding out
if we're as bad for each other
as we think we are
like smoke to a fire alarm
you'll stay up there
just out of my hands reach
in a room filled with people
at a punk gig
where we broke our bones for fun
like Icarus
too close to the sun

LIGHTS OUT

I waste too many words about when the lights go out
reading the tales from his skin with hungry hands
the bass and drum kit so loud in our ears
that reality couldn't yet roll off his tongue
in a basement bar where his smile
could be seen only in light intervals

but eventually the band will stop
and the hardest part will come around again
where we stare down at our feet
kicking around empty beer cups
its too quiet
morning light met almost with recoil
and a quick flash of lighters
while we suck in the air from last night
fearing the taste will disappear

with morning light
you become bubble gum blue
I hadn't even had the chance to get sick of the taste of you
before I had to spit you out
it's pouring with rain this morning
my boots are crushing my toes
my skin is sticky with sweat
in this come down

I tell enough stories about when the lights go out
and not enough about the light
but thats only because in the darkness
my body is a fortress of insomnia
all of those re run memories

beating the backs of my nocturnal eyelids
black and blue
until all I have left
is to count my burdens
like bullet holes in my skeleton
things I can hide only in the dark

but I guess we all have to wake up sometime
even with this aching in the side of my skull
the size of a black hole
dizzy and disorientated
I collide with you
I open my eyes
I panic naked to the daylight
to find his hands are holding mine steady

we're watching the pouring rain this morning
but today the natural light feels different
I'm awake to see reality for the first time in weeks
to see a sober view
for these shaking limbs
that have only seen empty streets
at 4am

SAD OR SORE?

I have souvenirs of pain
in the long deep pockets of a grey coat
bought years ago in Dublin
I let them mingle between my fingers
though I'd promised myself I would never look at them
again

I was wrong to think that something as
fickle as love or alcohol could stain
when there's such a thing as pain
and I'll admit somedays
its like standing bare foot in the snow
that familiar sting
that's only a shred of misery
nothing close to suffering

but on those cold December nights
they don't kiss
they bite
and its always when ice
makes its way into my lungs
becomes a kin
to the organs underneath my ribs
making a home in the blue veins
tracing their way under my skin

but back to November
back to the snow that has me clinging
to cigarettes between chapped lips
to the pain I need to water down
with whiskey drinking

too many nights spent
sending the wrong text
and hoping that when I wake up the next morning
that he wasn't there

and it's hard as fuck
being your own skeleton in the closet
the cold always haunts those bones
even when there is no longer skin to goose bump
but stuck in there next to the coats and old bottles of rum
I can smell that rage that clings
like the smell of copper on his skin

something that was bred into us
so that on our streets our prejudices were inherited
and became men built like oak trees
wearing clean suits
that they didn't have to go to court in
faces red with heat
where our fingers are still blue from
unpaid electricity bills
hands in pockets touching crisp notes
where our hands are clasped around coins given
hands shaking with guilt
but this storm is not yet winter
and I am so sick of talking
that I'll take up that empty bar stool
and the one next to me you are welcome to
because that's what the worn torn rage
leaking from his tongue told me to do
when I was sad or sore
or both

RED

she moves with the urgency
of her feet not being able
to keep up with her
or a pen scrolling too slow
across the page
for the words that are drawn
out of her mouth
why is everything pulling back
like her cheeks
scraped and dragged
across city streets
she is panic

she disappeared one night
after the sweat of a basement set
the night carried her away
till the next morning
where she was absorbing questions
her headache didn't have answers to
well she did
but the truth was in someone else's
bare skin
she is mistake

she hasn't slept in three days
she has smoked four cigarettes
in the past half hour out of a window
where work men in the construction site
have watched her get off

early in the morning
she is dripping glasses of wine into her system
un-phased by the notion of balance
when is enough just too much
she is grey

she never believed
in the meanings of dreams
but lately she has been dreaming
of the same forest
holding his hand
she scours for a belief in wandering
while she can't understand
how being in hell
feels like being unable to see anything
for the trees
she is lost

she is wild eyed with the chemicals
that regulate with her bloodstream
in the Barrowlands
while the ecstasy of the night sweats out of her pores
clinging to dark denim
she swears
she doesn't want to come back down yet
she is reckless

I'll break a kiss with you
you'll know exactly which one
when it happens
to see the sunshine break through me

all of these names
and more
are the shards of glass
that my body holds together
like remnants of a shattered window
that will slice you open
if you get too close

though I hope one day
I'll know if you bleed
red like I do

THE TRUTH

sometimes I'm scared
of telling the truth
whether that spawned
from rolling days
of un-rest
in a conflict
that gnawed on my skin
waiting for me to bleed
out the words
I wanted to say

on that note
don't start me on trust issues
when the only major plot lines
of the stories
from the year I was born
were skag and death
maybe I was born out of my
father's fear that he would wake
and I'd no longer be there

or of waiting in the car
staring down at the black and blue
bruises that met
the way the ocean met the shore
that reminded me of the
curly haired woman
with her head in her hands
that I wasn't good enough
for her
unless I swallowed the truth down

not that I lie often now
I just don't speak
when I'm supposed to
I let it fester in the creases of my eyes
hoping that when the question comes
the bite of my lip
the looking at my feet
and the furrow of my brow
wont give me away

before I'm ready to see the contortion
of hurt or confusion
on their faces
when the truth is exactly
what they didn't want to hear

or if I turned it on myself
when you still
kiss the memory
of someone who isn't me
as petty as it seems
it stuck there
like something sharp in my throat
I could barely swallow
and to this day
I'm still left with the bruise

but at least it was the truth

HEARTBREAK HOTEL

check in time
is whenever you'd like it to be
the neon sign
of a vacancy
has pulsed under my skin
for far too long maybe
but I tell myself
that the key in your hand
is exactly what I need

I wonder when this started
when you started treating
my body
like your own heartbreak hotel
hungry for whatever
sanctuary
it could give
or loneliness
it could forgive you of
even if it was temporary

this is just for the night
I told you again
so you don't bother to look
for cracks in the tiles
with your fingertips
overlook the stains
that will give my violent past
away

all you care about is that
the porn on the television
is working
and you can kiss my mouth
to taste the intoxication
you are craving
so you can forget
and treat my body
like you don't care about the deposit
just because the door was already
unlocked
when you got here

and in the morning
I will return to my body
from behind closed curtain eyes
from the corner
of my inner thighs street
that's been called lonely
far too many times
wondering if today
will be the day

that I turn off the vacancy sign
carry out the maintenance
on these fractured bones
and memories
like holes in the wall
I'm too used to fixing

this sounds like a cliche
to realise my worth doesn't
lie
the way I do
now carried in a creaking bathtub
where I scrub at
this self-hatred like blood
down the drain
I know it comes from my insides
but on some days
this body doesn't even feel like mine
to bleed

on others
I squeeze the key
into the palm of my fist
promising to never give
another piece of myself
to anyone else

SAINT OF BONES

do you think Saint Christopher
exists on nights like these?
I cling to the bronzed gold chain
around my throat
as I make my way through the inner city
and down another unfamiliar lane
I'm alone

I'm baptised in a cold sweat
and shaking from the change
of heat in the warehouse
as I stumble back
my eyes stinging from the strobe lights
begging for this place
I feel my way along the red stone
with scratched hands
guiding me through the East End
I've heard stories
about places like this
but I can't remember my own name
or how to be afraid

I'm alone
and clinging to a bronzed gold chain
when I see the house
alive and warm with bodies
I'm eager to be in between
I push the next day's regret
down in my stomach
where it brews with the come up
and becomes almost non existent
when I'm embraced by arms
I recognise

I think I eventually came to
when he touched my knee
a mishap of torn skinny jean knees
bumping one another
like bodies in a nightclub
and in a house like this
It's something we could have
or should have missed

but if I'm asked
even now I'll tell you
I still liked the way our bones
moved together
and how I found Saint Christopher
inside yours

ITCHY FEET

I don't believe much about dreams
surely chemicals aren't
functioning with higher consciousness
to send us a message
but lately
I've been dreaming about hotels
and strangers

I don't know when
I became this restless
but this seeping
red wine on cream carpet
skin feeling
it was quick enough
for me not to notice
but even now I can still
see the stain

see that I'm sick
and I'll only call myself that
because it gives me
the hope that there is a cure
rather than a weakness
in my brain

but for now this manifests
itself in my folding clothes
hand to fabric to suitcase

there's something cathartic
in the motion
that's replaced by nausea
when I run my hand across
the smooth wood of the door

to the steel handle
wrapped as tight as my white knuckles
clinging to my bag straps
and I wonder if you can run away wrong

after a few nights of this
obsessive pattern
I decided I didn't want to do this alone
I was sick of clasping room keys
and following strangers
up staircases
but how do you ask someone
to runaway with you
platonic or otherwise
what would I tell them?

the flash of a lingering outgoing message
to see who else might join me
caught between my fingers
over my eyes
words signed off
like an undecided suicide note
leave it all behind
runaway with me?
or am I saying that wrong
because who would admit to feeling this way

so maybe
this is just a daydream
and I'll leave it at that for now
let this be
words saved in a draft note
an ode to my itchy feet
and yours
if you happen to have them

TODAY

I can't write today
it's sunny
there's no wind and rain
to howl to my misery

I can't write today
because the milk in the fridge
for my morning coffee is still in date

I can't write today
when I wash my hands
waiting for the sting of bar work from the night before
I can't feel the cuts on my fingers

I can't write today
because I have no cigarettes or alcohol left
to poison my organs with

I can't write today
because none of the words would be true
I can't write today
because you left too

PROCRASTINATION

to sit barefoot
in front of a laptop screen
tips of my toes touching the chill from wooden panels
while I rest the weight of my twitching legs
on those blue toes
seemingly not noticing the shaking
at first

I glance out
of windows double my height
that kiss the ceiling
with strong shoulders to bear its weight
that I never had
and it's late

there is the soft hum of conspiracy theories
winding through a podcast
I stopped listening to
around the same time the frost
crept into the corners of the windows
escaping the sky that darkened
with the disappointment
of an unfulfilled day

casting down on
a bass left un-touched
a blank page staring me down
but being as stable as the dust
in the kitchen draft
I was aimlessly thrown around the house today
as fickle as Glasgow summers
and I thought
and thought
until sleep was the only witness to my failure

PLASTERS AND PAIN KILLERS

I keep packets of
plasters and painkillers
in the same top right hand side drawer
as my friend's obituary
sometimes the irony
still catches me off guard
or maybe this is my own
twisted metaphor
for healing
that I still haven't done yet

because its only ever fleeting
the way I stop smoking
cigarettes
when my chest infection returns
with a vengeance and a fever
and I cant stop seeing the things
I'd rather forget
so I let myself heal
if only for a little while before
I break what should be self-care
into a habit of self-destruction

a habit that originated
at the same time
as my early morning hangover wake up call
that I adapted to leave a house
before I hurt their feelings
the way I did the night before
when he asked me how many people
I had "been" with

and I told him I didn't know what he meant
did he mean physically?
or emotionally?
I'm not sure when I stopped believing
these were the same things for me

hopefully he wont notice I'm gone until its too late
too far out of range
for the collateral damage
I block out the memory of the one
of the last time I could regulate
anything close to love
because I've never been able to love
without casualties
not even him

one night
after serving a biker a drink
I leaned over the bar and asked him
does this rage ever go away?
he told me
that skin breaks and knuckles crumble
but anger is only pushed into silence
to assist the destruction
of my vital organs
that alcohol hasn't reached yet
I'm not sure what that reconciled for me

so the next time I woke
having missed the right side of the morning
all over again

What I Told Frank | 51

Frank handed me another cigarette
while I bundled into
an oversized grey coat bought years ago
in Dublin
one I hadn't worn in some time
but tonight felt right
under bridges
we followed the sound of each others
footsteps on uneven cobbles
to the place
that held the same painful irony
as the plasters and the pain killers

PEOPLE WATCHING

a creaking bar stool
kept their spines straight
while I ached
in the places between my shoulder blades
there was something sobering
about the low lights
the congregation of men in the corner
looking ready for a concrete slab
the smell of ales and spirits
mercilessly trying to cover the decay
that rested like dust in our chest cavities
though for some this is all they had

their eyes were worn out from wars
their shipyard past in the snarl on their lips
left abandoned yet like them still standing
the weather-beaten curve of their brow
always narrowed down

I leant against the bar
and wrote the story of the couple across the room
with a blunt fingernail on my thigh
leaving a welt to remind me
of the hatred in her eyes
while he stared off into the distance
his neck crooked against the booth
thinking of anyone that wasn't her
or a time when his hands on her
didn't end in disaster

my bloodshot eyes
begging for sleep that wouldn't come
wandered around the room
this place was the only stone walls
keeping us from wandering the streets
in an insomnia trance
the only black stout that would keep
me bedridden keep me deep in the grounds of sleep
let it touch my lips that were worn almost
from this residual practice

though soon we'd leave behind this shelter
in the cover of darkness
move beyond the dirty lanes
gutter's filled with alcohol and laughter
back to bed's with knurled bed posts
telling ourselves that the fire in our bellies
was warmer than sleeping alone

these tenements filled with noise through thin walls
built to store us away
when there was nowhere else to hold us down
but in red stone
this ice cold room where we could do it all again tomorrow
a ticking clock reminding us of the time we had
but for some of us this is all we had

FRANK

at night I tell the walls stories
so that in the morning
they can breathe my life back into me
the way the heat buries its way through the plaster
until it creaks
or maybe it will be bundled like old laundry in my arms
held with the same sickness
a scorned lover might

creasing it
each piece with last nights mistakes
laced with tobacco smoke and red lipstick
till I don't know the feeling of cotton tenderness
when I kiss
now that I have done it so often
all I can think of
is how warm and sloppy a mouth can feel
when all I want is for it to feel sincere

so it makes sense
that I met you drunk
pressed up against a wall in Audio
a barely finished drink in my hand
you told me that punk was back
and I could tell
from the raw of your throat
the way you stood in black denim and scars
that you were testament to that

I told you I liked punk rock
and you offered to show me some of your stuff
as we laughed at the couple in the corner
arguing and close to breaking point
you joked that hopefully one day
that would be us
and as drunk as we were
I wanted to believe you

instead
I told you about how much I hated my hands
that they were suffering now from alcohol related destruc-
tion
like arthritis that happened way too fast
and how I was jealous of yours
how they had created so much
yet I worried they could not carry the weight of those
worries

so I kept my hands in my pockets
training my lips to wrap around words
but I still kept stumbling over them
so I kept my voice in the pocket of my throat
and let your words like your fingers
wander up the back of my neck
to my ears

you told me that going by our sins
we would be born in the seediest pub in the city
slick with dirt and grime
dying like Bukowski
in badge ridden jackets
we would write poetry like punk songs

I said nothing
took another sip
you murmured something about
us in another life maybe
and wandered off
in search of another body
that would never know you like mines would
while I remained in my stronghold
of believing that this was the only way to protect
you from the fire in my belly
which meant only that I was toxic

I'VE NEVER BEEN GOOD AT PARTIES

I've never been good at parties
I'm the twitcher
wearing the same clothes
I wore to work last night
chain smoking outside
my heart beating
like something trapped under ice

begging for any hopes
of breathing again
while I pretend I'm not
breathing through the bottle
someone I know vaguely
handed me
to calm my electric
fairy light nerves
I panic everyone can see the glowing
under my pale skin

it'll give me away
that I'm not as relaxed
as my dripping candle wax lies say I am
so when they start passing
drugs around
I have to wonder whether
my heart can take the stimulant

I bail to the kitchen
which is too quiet for a normal party
fucking hipsters
taking up space in a bathtub instead
a few floors above my head

what happened to just drinking hard
with people you know
when did it become
how many people we could fit
in a cramped attic flat
whether we know them or not
for a press release of photographs
to prove we aren't alone

but I kept that to myself
while I drank dark rum
from someone else's bottle
hoping no one was sober enough to notice
I picked my way through people
like a murder mystery
narrowing my options down
when I came to think
the person who had invited me
hadn't even shown up yet

so I find the next
shaking victim to this house
and sit by them
he asked me what I knew about the city
I told him nothing
it looks different in the dark
the girl on my left agreed
and asked if it would be okay
to kiss me
saucer eyes made me hesitate
just as the doorbell rang
there was a pin drop silent response
because who the fuck rings doorbells anymore?

the shaking soul was the first
to answer the door
the most sober
but when it opened I sighed with relief
grabbed my coat
and followed Frank back out of the door

THE GAME

hangovers and come downs
aren't the only thing we have in common
Frank held my hand
as we rested our heads on a wall
our knees pulled up to our chests
in a room
neither of us knew very well

the last of the stragglers
haunted the room looking for leftovers
trying to roll cigarettes with less
than a pinch of tobacco
before they had to go
we could see from their eyes
they weren't ready to face the cold
and so far the owner of the house
was nowhere to be found

I stared over at him
he made my chest swell
with everything I had ever felt
so why did I only notice
the way Frank turned my hand
into the dominant hand shake
instead of the way his eyes focused on us
"I think I am a ghost"
I told Frank

my body was still here
but it was as if I could no longer see myself
that no one else could see me
I'm not sure what that kind of metaphor
says about my life choices
I just knew I didn't want to pick away at myself
until I wasn't a body anymore

there was reassurance that I found in Frank
that I hadn't seen in a long time
and that's the simplest way to explain Frank
as a person
Frank is all of my sin all of my mistakes
my anger and my violence
nirvana when all of this comes to a head
and I don't quite know how to fight it yet

my hand twists Frank's
till mine becomes the dominant hand shake
this lights a smile on Frank's face
the same way it does mine
we're both back in the game
that we've never played with anyone else

DECEMBER'S RESURRECTION

I left my underwear

> on your floor last night

a woman at work

> called me a slut

I told her if she did it more often

> maybe she wouldn't be so uptight

I promised after that

> to blunt my knife tongue

but I wont pretend

> my short burning coals temper

wont sharpen it again

I think I left them as a testament

> to my existence next to your bed

before I disappeared between

> the rounds of Christmas lights

and re-runs of X-Files that you left on

I think I was a different person then

  but she makes an appearance

from time to time

  like the shift from glances

at the start of the night

  to the smudged lipstick

at the end of it

I met Frank when

  I spent a year

being the smudged lipstick

  I wasn't ready to fix yet

so I can recognise when December

  just wont end

how she has been clawing

  her way through dirt to a resurrection

like Clark Kent

  this is a telephone box transformation

quick like the way she hit me

    on the subway

lay my head over the tiles and onto the track

    and said

"Frank sent me we need to talk"

But in my collection

    of confession tape words

I'll claim I'd never been there those weren't mine

    and I'd never saw her

even though now

    she has me

buried alive in winter

AFTER PARTY

the way Poe believed
windows were the eyes to the soul
I do too
I see mine sometimes
without recognising them
when I relay my age
over the top of the bar
to sleazy old men
they snarl I'm too young
to be this tired

so I'm not sure why I'm here
I tell them I've been to enough after parties
to know that I hate who I am
when I sink into them
but sleep is avoiding me
the way my eyes avoid anyone else
who might ask what I'm doing here
I'm hiding with the rain
a storm of thoughts
that are threatening this after party
like a hurricane

I try to set my story straight
in my head
where have I been tonight
where I plan to go in the morning
because last year I decided
to take days at a time
get through twenty four hours
again and again

so at midnight
I want to convince myself
I can tell a wine glass deep come back story
about this skeleton
wracked with wrangled nerves
squashed on a sofa next to people
just as lost

but that kind of ablution
will have to wait
it'll come when I wake up
I'll tell Frank everything
in one breath of honesty
reliving my sins
the crimes against myself
in one root sunk confession
as the branches of the truth
start to flower out of my mouth
though I'm not sure
what kind of graveyard regret
bouquet you'd arrange

it's new years day,
where whiskey kisses and morning
pretend they have just met
but this isn't a come back story
only because

I have not come back yet